7 petals

THERE IS ETERNITY...THERE IS POSSIBILITY

SIJI MANOJ THOMAS

I thank God Almighty
for His abundant blessings
that have shaped me into
who I am today.

Love you, Jesus.

This book is lovingly dedicated to
my mom and dad.

7 Petals

My book, **7 Petals**, conveys the essence of eternity—an eternity filled with endless possibilities.

The number 7 symbolizes spiritual growth, insight, and wisdom, guiding us to lead a life that is not only a blessing to ourselves but also to those around us. **Petals**, on the other hand, represent growth, completion, and the perfection of life's journey. They remind us of the fleeting nature of our time on Earth, inspiring us to spread joy, love, and beauty wherever we go.

The poems in this collection explore every facet of life—spirituality, emotions, love, joy, sorrow, and even death. As emotional beings, these experiences collectively define our humanity.

Let life be a journey of self-discovery, where we grow in harmony and find true meaning.

Contents

Pen is my power,
It express me through words.

After death engulfs; and my soul pass by,
I will live through my words –
Till the earth and the sun go by.

Brighter than the day –
Darker than the night,
Words guide me through
Whatever my plight.

Words are like flowers,
More the flowers bloom –
More my expressions groom.

Words are what make me glow,
It has the power; it made me grow.

My Journey

My writing journey began in 1999 when I moved to Mumbai from my hometown, Bhopal, for work. Residing in a working women's hostel, far from family and friends, I found myself in a new world, alone with my thoughts. During those quiet nights, I would sit on the hostel corridor floor, reading the Bible under dim lights, as room lights were to be switched off by 10 p.m. I often engaged in silent conversations with God, seeking solace and guidance. Gradually, my thoughts found a channel through words, becoming the fertile ground where the seeds of my reflections could blossom into life.

At first, my writings were simple conversations with God, recorded in both Hindi and English. Over time, my focus expanded to explore various aspects of human nature—my relationship with God, connections with people, and themes like love, friendship, old age, and death. I wrote about the emotions that define us: the pain of hurt, the weight of sorrow, the fleeting nature of happiness, and the resilience found in hardships. Many of my poems delve into life's challenges, reflecting on how the toughest trials offer the most profound lessons. These experiences made me stronger and gave me the courage to navigate life. I believe words, though silent, have the power to stir hearts and minds when they reach their audience.

I also find great inspiration in nature's beauty and am passionate about caring for stray animals and birds. One of my poems, My Furry Friend, was written in memory of a stray cat I cared for, who tragically passed away in an accident. Over the years, some of my works have been published in MTVEA Navi Mumbai Centre's magazine Seraph Voice in 2011 and 2019. Two of my Hindi poems were published in the book Mumbai ki Hindi Kaviyatriyaan in 2018. My bilingual book of quotes and poetry, The Wordchime - Silent and Resonant, featuring both English and Hindi, was published by YourQuote Publishing in 2023. I also write songs in Malayalam language. I enjoy expressing myself through singing and painting.

The presence of God has always been my greatest inspiration, enabling me to transform my thoughts into words. My poetry is not confined to a single emotion; it reflects whatever touches my heart and soul, shaping my thoughts into meaningful expressions. Before I begin any piece, I pray and thank God for His countless blessings, which continually guide my creativity.

I cherish moments of quiet observation, which allow my soul to create and connect. My life experiences have been my greatest teachers, shaping my growth as a person and a writer. Through words, I have found a way to share my journey, weaving my reflections into poetry that speaks from the depths of my soul.

I love the way I love.

I love being the way.

Siji Manoj Thomas

December 09, AD 2024

Mumbai

Acknowledgments

It brings me immense joy to acknowledge the presence and contributions of my loved ones who have walked alongside me on this beautiful journey of life. First and foremost, I thank God Almighty for His boundless grace and mercy, which have allowed me to achieve heights I never imagined possible.

With profound gratitude, I honor the unwavering love and selfless sacrifices of my parents, Mrs. Sosamma Thankachan and Mr. K.K. Thankachan. Their constant support and blessings have been the foundation of my life. They are my moral compass, my good fortune, and the essence of my being.

I am deeply indebted to my siblings, Ms. Sini Shaji and Dr. Ms. Ani Thankachan, for their love and steadfast presence in my life. They are my dedicated source of support. My journey would be incomplete without acknowledging the invaluable presence of my brother-in-law, Mr. Shaji P. Baby, whose unmatched support has been a treasure to our family. My nephews, Ishaan and Stefan, and my niece, Niyor, are the joyful sparks of my life. Their positivity and energy have been my antidote to life's challenges. I am also grateful for the blessings and presence of my in-laws throughout my life's journey.

To my beloved husband, Mr. Manoj Thomas — you are the foundation of my life. You hold my dreams in your heart and walk beside me through every moment. Your resilient support, quiet strength, and constant encouragement have enabled me to reach my highest potential. You are the rock that makes everything achievable, and for that, I am eternally thankful.

I also express my heartfelt thanks to my dear friend, Rashmi (Rash), who has brought joy, laughter, and goodness into my life. Our bond is eternal, and your presence has made my journey truly extraordinary. My gratitude also reaches out to my friends, relatives, church members, colleagues, and well-wishers, whose love and support have enriched my life over the years.

Finally, I want to acknowledge the soothing presence of my dear pets—Rosie, Goldie, and Blackie, along with Tikku and Akku. They hold a cherished spot in my heart and consistently fill my life with boundless love and joy.

To everyone whose presence has made a difference in my life, thank you for filling it with positivity, beauty, and meaning. With all my heart, I send you love and blessings. Today, I can proudly and joyfully exclaim, Hurrah! I am here!

Much love and gratitude to all.

The First Petal –

Singing Soul

1. Our Secret Shrine

The flowers know
How delicate the feeling.
The rivers perceive
What drives it through.
It's nature so profound and pure,
The breathtaking feeling of LOVE for sure.

When finally, the heart and soul matter,
Even if; the world around shatter,
All in its uniqueness and bonding
Where nothing more is left wanting.

If its love; it's the unexplained,
It manages the stage pretty.
Universe and me perpetual and mine,
Well-guarded in our secret shrine.

Love doesn't have synonyms,
It is what it is.
Ride through this storm and calm,
And let your soul sing a psalm.

2. Happiness that Meant Life

The more we were apart
The more we became a part.
It's just a feeling that made us close
It made us happy at what we chose.

Fullness in those moments
And pretty the smile,
Gripping the fragrance
Mesmerizing embrace.

The walk with you seemed so short
A voyage, I never wished to abort,
You made a space for yourself
At a sweet corner, in my heart.

Your simplicity makes you charming
Your being makes you appealing.
You are just exceptional
Made me grand too special.

Moments spent are beauty beyond
World and I are nowhere found
To an emotion that reels in you –
That I am somewhere there in you.

3. Like the Fire there is None

There is spark in me
There is beauty in me
There's fire in me; I am love,
Both big and small
And the mighty and low
A fire in my being; I aglow.

It's powerful and bright
Wipes dark and is light
There's fire in me; I am love,
All the world it renews
Wherever way it goes
Creation comes alive; I aglow.

All the elements are one
Like the fire there is none
There's fire in me; I am love,
No more doubt have I
When the life goes by
Abounding and pure; I aglow.

There is fire in my heart
The joy in its beat
There's fire in me; I am love,
Its presence is God
And its absence is dark
There's fire in me; I aglow.

4. I will Wait Lord

I will wait Lord

To see Your divine aura.

I will wait Lord

To live the happiness, You sew for me.

I will wait Lord

To see my wounds healed at last.

I will wait Lord

To close my eyes in Your arms.

Come what may – I will live,

Though not enough – I will give.

I walk on thorns that pierce my heart

Yet, I smile deceive my pain,

I know Lord; You are waiting for me

With Your arms as garland for me.

5. Being to Care

It's God's grace that I walk
It's God's blessing that I talk,
It's God's presence that I see
It's God's love what I feel.

It's God's gift whatever I got,
It's God's plan; whatever I achieve.

I live to feel His love,
I live to be a blessing.

Life sometime behaves strange,
But that's how our Lord arrange.

It's not tough to smile and share.
It's our being to love and care.

6. A Priced Pearl

It's not that I am weak
Rather it's my strength that's dripping,
The fighting spirit; that made me able
Left me behind, for its journey ahead.

Struggling alone amid nowhere
I gather the pieces of my past.
No rains will ever make me green,
No winters will ever make me chill.

All of it…just timelines –
Wherefrom I watch life; pass by
Tons of memory I carry,
Dragging my spirit all the way.

All that's pink is not for me
All the bruises now I hide
Tell me…where it went haywire?
Now I know…what's more in store.

I pull apart all my strings
Yet I hear it loud and out.
Though He made me tender and weak
His outright power covers me firm,
That one day; I'll shine as a priced pearl
Calm like the moon…sparkling like a star.

The Second Petal –
Beyond Words

7. In Every Lifetime I Meet You

The summer springs

The cuckoo sings,

The winter white

The icy delight.

In every season

We choose a reason

To mingle with joy and love,

To spring on the cloud above,

To greet and sing a song anew.

In all my phases I greet you

In every lifetime I meet you

Beyond the sparkle of stars

Beneath the glistening of dew,

Something is there

That I wish to share,

Why to shy now

The time is here now.

Over the years –

That I met you

As the times have passed,

I have become more you.
In all my phases I greet you
In every lifetime I meet you

Every road has an end
Every dream a destination
Being near or far
Is not what matters,
It's the way we make
When we close our eyes,
Even my heart – it beats for you.
In all my phases I greet you
In every lifetime I meet you

Let's soar to the highest heaven
Let's watch the world pass by,
No one waiting for us
Not even we; yearning for something.
Let time stand still
Let our breath be at rest;
Let the light of love cover us
Let love bond me and you.
In all my phases I greet you
In every lifetime I meet you

8. A Magical Impact

Whenever it's that time to leave
Whenever it's that time for byes,
A moment comes with no comeback
Though in pain, yet we smile.

Silently our mind readies to feel
The pain a flower feels when plucked
Yet it doesn't fail to offer aroma –
And lo! It creates a magical impact.

What you gave is a gift for life
Though now never, yet forever.
Prayers and good wishes come your way
You be as you are, now come what may.

It's that time when speech is silent
It's that time when the silence speaks,
Life realizes it has to move on
Bonds promise they have to stick on.

The verdict of life is crystal clear
It never guarantees now and near,
Though far away like miles and space
Yet nearby like; smiles and embrace.

9. It's You Who Keep Me Safe

In this world of constant fear;
When destination not so clear
Each moment I look up to You
Coz, it's You who keep me safe.

Why the burden do I carry?
When I know the Lord will bear
All anxiety I pour unto You
Coz, it's You who keep me safe.

All the pain that tax our minds
And the sorrows crossing hearts
On the cross the Savior beared it all;
Coz, it's You who keep me safe.

Why Oh! heart, you're so lonely
Why so bothered Oh! my soul,
His power and promise stride in us
Coz, it's You who keep me safe.

Hear the archangels sing;
And see His aura bright,
No more doubt across I carry
Coz, it's You who keep me safe.

10. Now I am Me

There comes a time

When neither you're glad nor sad,

When time just moves on

Without even knowing you.

No emotions are felt affecting

You are carrying you and self

And nowhere you reach.

Breath is your master

And silence your partner,

Speed doesn't matter

As I am not in any race.

I don't mind being let down

As now no one's bothered,

And now; not me either.

It's easy to be carried away
Where the mind drives,
Be steady; stay.
Nowhere have you come from
And to nowhere you go.
Time is moving
And I'm finding me along.

People came; now in memories live,
Good my heart's a paradise.
Where the chimney smokes
And life is alive.

It doesn't matter if –
I am scorned
Or taken for granted,
Or feelings are bruised
Now I don't exist in their presence.

Now its fine with me
This is me.
Now I am me.

11. Through My Eyes

It's already planned,
Before I had breath.

This life
Through my eyes,
So wonderful.

But I see –
Within is a scream;
And teary my eyes.

Where's the horizon
That gives peace –
And hears the unheard.

I carry myself
From shore to sea,
Vastness engulfed
Resembling my tears.

Marvelous this journey
Still beating on rhythm,
Dancing the tune.

My hope doesn't die
My heart will win
Seeing all happiness
I too will smile.

All boundaries crossed
Overcame all twinge,
As love filled my soul –
Now will wrap me whole.

12. Whence It Came from, Whence will It End

Today again I had the passing feeling
Today again I feel I am not among alive.
There unnoticed; life goes by
I watch my path, feeling the breeze.

Whence it came from
Whence will it end
No more the sun shines;
No more the star spark,
Beneath the darkest valley
Not even my shadow nearer.
Eyes open or never
Doesn't matter now.
It's all the same
Both life; and other.

I'll never ask – why me
No questions remain,
No answers prevail,
Covering my soul –
My being is burdened
My breath reminds me
That life needs me.

Whence it came from
Whence will it end

Smiles are mere pick-up stories
Prompt I manage my days to the end.
What lay beneath the soul –
Remains alive with my breath.

Whence it came from
Whence will it end
I know not, what will come through
Astounded I am – I came this long.

The Third Petal –
Chaos Within

13. The Windblown Leaf

Years fading like gushing waves
Gone are smiles and happy days;
What more to be sad of
What more to be glad of.

I flutter like a windblown leaf
Covered is my skin with dust and web;
Dry is my marrow and bones feeble
No amount of water could nourish me ever.

Where not a speck of sun enters
Nor does moonlight shine on me;
I found a place in darkness and sorrow –
Where I see – neither me nor my shadow.

It doesn't matter –
If it's morning, noon or night;
If it's something wrong or right,
Shackles clutch me tighter and tight
No one to hear my sorrow and plight.

14. As this was Meant to Be

A million times love tried me
Was it for me, or isn't for me.
Tears rolled down
That I didn't try to wipe
As this was meant to be,
Let it be so.

Why on grass I stepped on thorns
Stood a while bleeding hard,
The pain pierced; did hurt my heart
Peace, no goodness can ever grant.
Wounded my heart, wounded my soul
Lost in myself; not found anymore.
Was it like; I didn't deserve it
Or like; it didn't deserve me.
As this was meant to be,
Let it be so.

Often love's not a vibrant blossom

Comes betrayal and pain with it

For some it's pure magic –

For rest, a terrible tragic.

Gather up till you are alive

Look up to memories, till you survive.

It's okay if I did walk alone

I thank God; He did make me walk.

As this was meant to be,

Let it be so.

15. How Much More to Carry?

As the sun rise
Darkness befalls on me,
Sharp lights blind my eye
Nothing can I see – nothing can I see.

I wander in this scenic world
With my own set of sorrows and fright,
In silent pain; life pass by,
Nothing do I gain – nothing do I gain.

My faith turned to grief unbound
More of this life means shattered dreams,
No more words to express pain,
No more smiles – no more smiles.

More and more blows fall on me
Like a prisoner I cover my wound
Tears and blood flow hurting my soul,
Nobody to seek – nobody to seek.

What I got; well deserving it was.

How much more to carry?

Weak and fragile I feel;

Broken hearted my heart aches,

Withered away life – withered away life.

16. The Winter Night

Devastating this silence
Turbulence these tears.

Wayward my life wander;
In valleys where darkness abides.

Nothing good came through
Silently my life goes by.

What more is left to bear
Tired and hurt –
My shoulders feel heavy.

Alone I walk in the winter night;
Where not even one, is in my sight.

Wind blows that make me chill,
Frightening my way
Nothing more, is left to say.

17. Rhythm of My Heart

In all walks of life
Had God being with me
Never in my life –
Was I left alone.
Never in my years –
Did I feel alone.

As the years passed
More my faith and love increased
Never felt; I craved for a need
Received all on a perfect occasion.

Was confident in all my misfortunes
Overcame struggle with His power;
Was a blessing for near and far
God is good and loved me dear.

All I have now –
A beating heart with no rhythm
A wounded soul and tearful eyes.
Downcast and dejected I am
Everyone I have, yet lonely I am.

Now, my God's not with me
He's busy with others in town;
He never ears my prayers even
Like am long; forgotten for Him.

It's been years He heard me
Days are out of count,
Nothing more of me alive now
Nothing more of me wanting now.

The burden of breath carry I can't
Weighed down being alive
More I want God be near
More He isn't ready to hear.

Broken to bits now is my life
Feels like I am walking dead
No more meaning in smile or tear
No more reason to be far or near.

God exists – for sure – but not for me
Gone are the days that He cared for me,
Walking alone all my days; till I am gone
This the way I'm left – forgotten and forlorn.

18. Just Leave Me So

Now I am tired
Smile and silent
Survive will I…
But life gone by.

Sad for me
Happy for self,
Nothing is what I brought
Nothing is what I got.

No more galore in my days,
No more dreams get to gaze.
Wandering in midst of shattered pain
Naught under the sun I wish to gain.

Poles apart are sunrise and me
Till afar off is darkness I see;
Stuck together is me and sorrow
A speck of smile…let me borrow

I shouldn't ask You why
I wouldn't ask You why
I felt, I was special for You
Now I feel; I do am.

Words now have started failing me
Distress now has begun trailing me,
Behold my being – is none for You,
Behold my soul – I pity for you.

The battle of life is what I fought
The battle of life is what I lost.
Barren sweats grip me tight
Lonely I tremble, scarred with fright.

Soul and I wounded for life
Closing my eyes, just leave me so.
Closing my eyes, just leave me so.

19. Invisible Presence

I'm special for them
And I'm invited
But my shackled heart
Never lets me in.

All the occasions and smiles
Felt like I'm none again.
Broken and torn my breath
Smiling for them again.

I'm present with them,
But invisible
I'm treated fair
Joyfully holding despair.

The freshness of the dark,
And my silent mind
Nothing I perceive
Struggling for the beam.

I'm here…there too
Witnessing it all –
There from my carved corner,
Smiling through, managing all.

The Fourth Petal –
Eternal Strength

20. A Thousand Times

Oh! Lord

A thousand times came the rain
But I carried an umbrella.

A thousand times did the roses bloom
Oh! I didn't feel their aroma.

A thousand times did the cuckoo sing
Yet, I didn't bother to listen.

A thousand times I laughed out loud
But my Lord missed my smile.

A thousand times the sun rose;
A thousand times the moon,
I saw…yet wasn't aware.

May my coming times be different, from those thousand times,
May God bless me…not a hundred, but a thousand times.

Not a hundred, but a thousand times.

21. Not We, but One in Him

Like the brilliance of a million stars
Was born a King in the shadows of dark.

Came to this world to be the way
And achieved it, in His own way.

Some followed His views and hoped His help
He taught to pray and keep the faith.

He is with us in our distress and sorrow
He gave us joy which none could borrow.

He suffered pain and torture
Like a sinner and a lawbreaker,
He gave us eternal life
Being a friend and a good teacher.

Came to this world and fulfilled the Word
Left this space with a promise to return.

His love is with us that we may go on

Being with Him feels great at heart,

His love and passion, are rest apart.

Understand Him – Love Him,

Join Him – keep faith in Him.

He gave us everything

With nothing in bargain,

So, we remain in Him

Not we, but one in Him.

22. His Abiding Love

When God gives me heed
Nothing more for I greed
He provides me forever –
With all that I need.

His eternal love fills my view,
It's fresh like, the morning dew.

In my trouble He covers me,
In my pain He delivers me.

When my heart grieves
He feels my pain.
When my eyes weep,
He says – 'never again.'

His presence walks with me
His love cares for me,
He knows that I am weak
He helps me conquer the highest peak.

I am forever His own,
A bond He will never disown
How far my life moves on –
He guides and makes to carry on.

This beautiful creation
He gifted us
His abundant grace
He showered on us
His life too…He gave for us
Defeated death and alive in us.

You filled my life with the beauty of love
You gave my life the essence of being,
Your abiding love lights it all
Holding me tight whenever I fall.

Thank you, Lord, for reaching me this far
Lead me through, till I reach the skies afar.

23. The Lord is My Shepherd

How difficult my times might be
How sorrowful, my steps may be,
No matter, how hard my life tries me
I have faith – my Lord is beside me.

Even if green pastures turn to parched ones
Even if sorrows become ever weary,
Even when; nothing seems to console our heart
The Lord is my Shepherd and I shall not want.

In His arms, I am safe
His amazing smile heals my wound;
His tender touch soothes my weariness,
His love – makes me forget; all my sorrow.
He is my only support and help
With Him I sustain,
Through Him I gain.
He is the bread for my body
He is the breath of my life,
He is what – I earned
It is with Him that I gained.

He's the sight of my eyes
He's the life of my being,
He is the melody to my song
My heart yearns to sing His praise.

His silent nature gives me patience
His powerful speech gives me might,
Blessings and blessings surround me
His untiring love and care adorn me.

I discovered Him within me
His right hand forever leads me,
Although my path be treacherous –
With Him my destination reaps riches.

In this world of unpredictable changes
How wonderfully my life He manages,
His unmatched love for me is unparalleled
It's so priced to say – The Lord is my Shepherd.

24. Where the Sky Ends

All the Heavens declare His glory
Beautiful and magnificent His story,
Singing songs and psalms to Him aloud
All glory and honor to Christ my Lord.

No trouble or sorrow near
No more Satan to fear
Walking the clouds with my Lord
Like a child my eyes behold.

Higher and higher my mind soars;
All my burden my Lord bears
He loves me like I am the only one
He is with me till I am set and done.

Joy and peace in the air
His might the angels declare,
A place we desire to be in
Where the love of God fills in.

Sitting on the throne of praises
Adorning the crown of love,
It's where all the hearts mend
He's there where the sky ends.

25. The Truth Abides in Me

His treasures abound
Mighty His power,
Radiant this earth He made
Vast this sky as shade.

I'm happy in every walk
Coz, He holds my hand,
In everything I see You
Calmness in my being I feel.

From the mountains that rule
To the mighty seas below,
Wondrous His glory
His breath in every form.

Reception that He gave
Is the love that I receive.
It's You that is in all
You're the only truth –
That abides in me.

August His works,
Unimaginable His creation,
Beautiful I'm coz beautiful Thou art;
You're with me –
Even though my soul departs.

Every word I hear; I hear You
Everything I see; I see You
Every breath I take; I feel You
Every song I sing, Thou art tune
Your love I feel, coz Thou art love.

Every bit covered in Your aura,
Nature's blessed with Your plethora.

The Fifth Petal – Transcending Life

26. On the Other Side

The one who makes me smile
It is You…it is You…it is You.
The one who makes me mine
It is You…it is You…it is You.

Though darkness befalls on me
Your shine; makes my path glow.

This, I learnt from my years
The one who walks along are tears,
Alone I walk through this
Alone I…Alone I.

Friends are there for you
But where's the one who's for you.
But I found You Lord, back on those paths,
On the day, when I was broken and torn.

Lord said, behold; I am there for you
No matter what…no matter how.
Even if things turn out…for better or for worse.

We will stick together,

Till we pass through these times,

On the other side too; when we do meet

Let be a celebration that forever chimes.

27. Death – A Silent Winner

It can't be said – How?
It can't be explained – Why?
A belief like anonymity
A conviction like mystery.

Whatever bliss it brings
It accompanies its grief along;
Everyone is a partaker
In it there's no exception.

Sometimes it's sudden
Other way it drags us long.
What on earth the route we choose,
The end is forever in its arms.

A meeting fixed for a day to come
A permanent finish to life become,
A silent winner in all prospects
Unexplained truth in all respects.

28. The Last Apple

When it's time to leave
Even if pending to give;
No matter dreams remain
Without me; lives sustain.

Thought tomorrow would be mine
Blessed with; the bread and wine
Neither tomorrow came –
Nor I; able to breathe again.

Didn't have I a bit of notion
Diligent life full of commotion,
What was mine; wasn't mine
Now Son of Man; nearer shine.

Closing my eyes afar I fly
Tears of relief cover my eye,
Now that all is set and done
Life for me; has just begun.

Before final adios

Saw beside my fort –

Hey! Did I miss you before my grapple?

Oh! Indeed; you are my last apple.

29. Our Unseen Fate

Life is like a slow poison
Each second nearing death
However, tough life makes you feel
It feels bliss in the arms of death.

All our days are numbered
We can never escape our unseen fate
Ultimately, from the deep abyss of life's prison
We find freedom from the shackles of being.

If life's a celebration –
And endless bound of joy
Death, its image
Might enfold some delights.
When life rules
We never feel life alive;
Death renders understanding
How precious being on this side.

Death, acts as a shrine to us
Where we meet our divine in person,
Though how tough a life we had
There our soul gets to rest.

However grand life might be
Death on time, breaks the guard.

It doesn't matter how decked our presence is
What matters finally, is how beautiful our soul is.

30. My Furry Friend

Without calling for her
She walked towards me
Climbing the steps; nearing me
I thought she's just taking her time,
Then I saw her half – cut limb
A terror of shock waved me through
Eyes not ready to believe it
And heart, not willing to take it.

I saw –
Each passing day giving her suffering
She might have dreaded being alive
She would lose her one limb;
But I prayed – her life be spared.

I love her so much
Now, I wish this ends;
My tears and prayers didn't get her relief
With passing hours, she was tortured to death.
She was alive – but was still…
Roaming ants devouring her bit by bit
Eyes closed – but ears alert
Heart was pounding; but to no avail
Her life was at rest – yet alive.

Her five days of ordeal,
Came to a silent end.

Her masked face with twin colors
Her transparent eyes full of twinkle
She brought sparkle whenever I met her
She felt love whenever I touched her.

Gone are the days I saw her
Gone are the times I touched her,
Never again will I ever see her
My memories will always house her.

31. It Always had Been Me

Troubles and trials
Always find destination me,
Now it's better to have them
Rather having smile in bits.

With loneliness my luggage;
Tears being my walking stick,
Alone I travel the path of life
Following the sunshine and shade.

No more questions to ask
No more answers to seek,
How much my heart can weigh
How much my soul can tear?

A deafening silence talks to me
A unique relation beyond words.
Now no word hurts me,
Now no relation needs me.

Not even death will gather a crowd
Not even one will cry out loud,
It was I who cried, when I joined here
Let it be so, when I depart the sphere.

The Sixth Petal –
Pinnacle of Aura

32. The Half Voyage

The curtain raised
The spectacle began,
The characters sharp
Tuning melody and harp.

The autumn did leave –
So did the summer come;
Fate has blessings for many
But it's gracious on some.

Though it was short;
The journey was sweet,
Feels like yesterday
But months flew by.

It would have been better
If it was meant for more,
As destiny's the magician
It did turn magical.

Not desiring for anything much
Only so…we keep in touch.

33. Rise and Cruise

You did receive the utmost of love
You did live in the pinnacle of aura;
You did taste the height of success
Now what more, now what next.

Life doesn't need; any boundaries to be safe;
Let it fly like an eagle, and dash against the rocks.
Nothing can stop you; from being the you
Get ready to scramble; and skip the queue.

Recreate your parameters
Rise above your precincts,
Leave behind what confines you
Live your dream that drives you.
Neither you're here nor there
You're now and everywhere.

Feel the life in every breath
You're the source, you're beautiful
Let the speculations rest a while
Greet life anew; and share a smile.

You might fall, yet rise and cruise
Be your partner, saunter the shore,
Even though the world shatter around
Gather your bits; let love surround
Amidst the sparkle, beguiling pearl you're
Nothing more desiring, genuine rare you're.

34. The Oneness

Like a wind chime
Silent and resonant,
A little wind wave
And becomes a divine tune.

Sometimes strong,
Sometimes mild.
When silence engulfs
Unnoticed it goes.

Made with
The thread of bonding
The wood of affection,
Adorned with Crystals and;
Beads of love.
It depicts…
The oneness of sound and silence.

Its sound serene.
Its silence heavenly.

35. Gentle Breeze, Turbulent Storms

I am ready to clutch the days
In a fearless and noble way
To achieve a new spark day by day,
To reach a new streak in every way.

Some feel its gentle breeze
Others get; turbulent storms
So, pleasing this substance –
How melodious the momentum.

All the people we meet
And the bonds we make,
Are tough ways learnt
Not meant to regret.

Life is never a mystery
All our being, a set up story,
To go on is what it tells us
Only till the time it needs us.

Steering through its valleys

Gorging along the pathways;

Stumbling and then regaining again

Reaching the horizon admiring the blue.

36. Wings of Love

When it's tough for me
He lets me through
Blessings and blessings;
I accrue with You.

Special I am
He made me so;
Broken was I
He mended me so.

Vulnerable I am
He's my strength
Poor I am
He's my wealth
Failed have I
He's my hope
Trying to limits I am
He helps me cope.

He's the freedom

I strive for

With His wings of love

To afar skies I'll soar.

37. His Love Surround

Stars witnessed His birth
Winds came to a silent calm
What a precious moment it was,
What a blessed life we have.

Shining like the morning star
Greeting with a pleasant smile;
Love is the lesson He taught
Peace; the message He brought.

Shepherds gathered to greet Him
From afar the kings came;
What a splendid aura He had
What a blessed life we have.

He came to save us from our sin
And to show the way of God;
He's with us, for now and beyond
Smile your tears, let love surround.

38. I have Reached

When even joy,
the sorrow doesn't feel,
I have reached.

If I don't realize
being me anymore,
I have reached.

I don't match with greens
the blues;
and the darkness vast,
I have reached.

Nothing to borrow
Nothing though I gain.
I smile throughout,
Yet, I suffer pain.
Is this what life really is –
Then, no more I am game.

I am still

I react not.

Not even I to reach heavens or other

As now, I already am.

This is now what is of me

I don't remain.

All in me

I in all.

Yes, I have come a long way

Yes, I have reached.

39. Treasure Unlocked

There is a smile beyond this pain
There is treasure to be unlocked,
All over I find tears of joy
Now I need a reason to smile.

What is it that blocks my way?
Isn't it time to clear and sway
How I long to be in suite
Let me be, the same as they.

My mind's a mirror for You,
All clear where nothing's hidden
Refine your temple in a grand way
That life comes and live Your way.

My faith in You gave me honor till date,
Whatever I needed came to my gate.

The Seventh Petal – *Shadow of My Heart*

40. Beneath the Overpass

The road over the depths
I and the breeze partners in ride,
Music is loud and the journey is set
Enjoying the speed, forgetting the rest.

One day I took the road below,
There I saw; lives survive.
Come sun or moon –
All invited around.

Thinking faces; what next to do,
Uncombed hair; no dreams remain,
Vehicles pass by, their faces still
Daily struggles and tears along.

I stand there; sojourn and silent
Blank and patient; wearing a sigh.
I reached out, they crowd me over
As though I was a form beyond.
Here I found the human in me,
Closing my mind, hearing them out.

Afar somewhere a song is playing
Kids under the sun; brows sweating.
Men thinking of tomorrow
And women, what dinner to cook.
Rags and litter over and around
And they live, as nothing beyond.

Nothing's permanent in the temporary
Watching the stars, dreaming galaxy,
Lives endure in these shadows dark,
Living their dreams to make a mark.

41. Together with Myself

Time is the perpetrator
And I'm being sentenced.
Disabled even to flutter my wings
Sad, I sit, in the murky corner.

Chirping birds comfort me
Dew drops water my soul;
Only I and my tears remain
One with none now.

Silently I witness –
Few completed their term;
Will start anew.
I just stood and stared –
Coz I've been sentenced for life.

No solace from anywhere
Wounded my being, alive still.
Only words remain tied with me
Binding me together with myself.

All that was in me
I have given in full,
Nothing more that was me
Now do remain in me.

I tread the valleys –
Of my soul divine,
You're an angel –
Now, you are mine.

42. Begin with Yourself

All that's beautiful
All that's charming
Far from me
Though, I near.

Don't have anyone to blame
Just me and me…always been me,
Going the ways, where life takes
Even though, my heart pains.

The cycle of life goes on
With reasons to cheer and grow;
What more is me wanting for
What more of me am waiting for.

I'm like that cornered stone
Like that shady grown tree,
Just seasons pass by
Just life goes by;
And the scorching sun
Melting my heart.

An outing with joy as my date
A serving that wasn't on my plate;
It's never late to begin with oneself
True beauty lies to begin with yourself.

43. It's Life that Matters

Sometimes you must be on your own,

You yourself; have to re-pair your soul to your being,

No medicine can work miracles

Only your heart can heal you.

Even time fly past;

Nothing or anything rests with you,

You are calm, but inside you churn

For what more shall you wait.

All the glory has become a story

Even my own self is slipping through,

Only one destination is for me to reach

Where there remain no more goodbyes,

It's not just a matter of time

Its life that matters.

Not always can a smile rescue you
Sometimes only tears care for you,
And you try so hard to manage
And to nowhere you reach.
Pondering with yourself and memories
If it had happened the other way round
Even then; it would have been so.

Came to this world on a set date
Walking along dreaming the sky,
I did my best and won my heart
Even though; the world I failed.
Oh! my soul, it's my best I gave,
I have reached, now let me rest.
Let me be me,
Forever so engulfed in me.

44. Hope...It's in Me

On a sunny day, when everything seems bright

All of it; so properly placed

All the roads; easily traced

Being what we are, is all positivity

All so wonderful; so poised

Even twitches handled easy.

Hope – It's in me…Its there within me

But when times are overshadowed

Something in me starts draining,

Dark murky corners of my mind

Start taking the center stage.

All that was making me beam

Looks gloomy demean.

All the strings too; become downbeat

All the earth; becomes off-hand.

Hope – was it really there? Where's it now?

Where am I now?

Why all that I see, is not, what I want to see

Where's gone all my limitlessness?

Where's gone all my times…that were on the maximum?

In this time of distress, when eye sees only stress,

I know where I ought to look

To make straight all that's bend.

I closed my eyes…I felt it within me,

Somewhere it went hiding

When I was busy with my descend.

Again, a spark found space in me

Its aura bright shone in me

Its I who should do it…Its I who should believe it

Amid a million stars

The moon is what we look for,

Do focus on what we are made of.

Our eyes may not see it

Our minds can envisage it.

Oh! my being, be rest assured

Its within you.

It's not elsewhere – it's there in you.

When we pray – it's hope.
When we dream – it's hope.
When we love – it's hope.
We are alive – it's hope.
If there's hope, there's tomorrow,
If no…then our today's just a dream.

Hope
It's what you're made of
Hope
It's what make you live
Hope
It's what make you strive

Never let go of –
Hope.

45. I Know How It Feels…When the Sun Sets

I ain't alone

I am with me.

I never left me on its own

Coz, I know how it feels when the sun sets.

Even though it's tough to comprehend

I am now at ease with me and myself,

The toughest of challenges can't fail me now

I am my family. I am with me now.

When it's the season of sorrows

Its always with me, that it flourishes.

Even in the crowd of millions

I am always the easy catch.

Even though I crossed decades

Yet it spots me clear.

Wherever I am

It drags me near.

Be it sunshine or moonshine

I am the one, who carries it through,
Bundles and bundles; it burdens me low
It tries to strain; I manage somehow.

Tears are pleasing now
The only reality I carry now,
Alone I with me; or in a crowd
Never am I with someone I found.
Neither am I alive; nor am I life
He pours His breath; and I feel His earth.
There's nothing more left to sustain
Though I am one; yet I contain.

Pixels of beauty surround me tight
Life took left; others took right,
I am the one who bears it high
I am the one who hears my sigh.
Never I sensed what it feels and how
Broken and fretful it reels me now.

46. I Don't Care what the World Cares

It's not for the world to decide
Whether you won or what you missed.
It's not for the world to judge
Whether you lived by its standards.
Rather, it is you who is to dwell,
It is you who is to decide.

Nobody cares,
Whether you are alive or gone,
Till the time you are someone, it works
But, when you are in shadows, you are none.
Even though love surround you
Keep it to heart; one day you will be your own,
All the palaces and horses rendered meaningless
Yet, the sun shine and the moon glow.

Now, steer through and set for stroll

Feel the breeze against your soul.

Nothing more precious than this bond

When you're one with your own and none.

Cherish this moment and do what it takes

Now, I don't care what the world cares.

47. The Lonely Absence

Life is tough in every phase
Bit tougher when getting old
Even tougher when no one's by your side
You yourself present in the lonely absence.
Why all this pain one has to suffer?
Why doesn't this end in just one go?

Why it has to take an epoch?
He observes this suffering meant on one
When He knows it's way too much
The presence of bonds too; feels cyclic,
Not much of either emotion is tolerable
Alas! And what to say about pain.

I too not with them
In their grey days
Learnt; one has to be on his own.
All the terrible aches
Come together as one.
No balm of any use
Just suffering that gets gross
No more dew to wet the moss.
Delicate we become
And harsh the immediate
Though tired and drained
Alas! The breath clings on!

Grief, I hear in their voice
Miles apart I sit and wonder
No one and nothing can transform it
It's the deal of life that they live in.
Purpose and meanings all long gone
The vase shattered; the flowers dried.

What they did; they reap
What I; I will
The wind's blowing
The birds chirping
Alive I am.
Alive they are.

48. Now I am One

Now I am One
Me and the Sun,
The stars are me
The Moon is mine.
Wherever I go,
There I shine.

The leaves sing
The greens are me,
Pearls of dew
And the air I breathe.
Together with me
Forever I am.

Clear is the sky;
Clouds see I fly,
Nothing to stop me,
To the ends I reach.

Now I am none,
Now I am One.

About the Book

This book holds a part of my essence. As you read, you will discover a rich tapestry of our shared existence interwoven throughout its pages. It will guide you to feel a connection with the Universe and help you embrace the unfolding of life's moments. Living with authenticity and truth is the essence of what life truly means.

As you journey through the poetry, I believe it will resonate deeply with you, and you will see reflections of yourself in the verses.

We are created to reign, even in the face of failure.

About the Author

Siji Manoj Thomas, resides in Mumbai, holds a Commerce degree and a Masters in Social Work. A passionate poet, she finds inspiration in nature, emotions, and the intricacies of human relationships, crafting narratives that deeply resonate with readers. Her talent lies in exploring profound themes with grace and simplicity, leaving a lasting impact. Her book, 7 Petals, embodies her gift for weaving poignant reflections, inviting readers on a journey of life, growth, and self-discovery.